Animals on the Farm

Élisabeth de Lambilly-Bresson

GARETH**STEVENS**

PUBLISHING

A Member of the WRC Media Family of Companies

The Rooster

I am a rooster.
Because I am king
of the farmyard,
I have a red crown
and fancy feathers.
At daybreak,
I sound the wake-up call.
Cock-a-doodle-doo!

The Pig

I am a pig.
I love to eat grass.
I love corn and potatoes, too.
Most of all,
I love to roll in the mud!
Oink! Oink!

The Cow

I am a cow.
I walk in the fields all day.
I eat grass to make
good milk for you.
I walk and eat
and chew and chew.
Moo! Moo!

The Duck

I am a duck.
Thanks to my webbed feet,
I swim very well.
My feathers are like a raincoat,
and they keep me
very nice and warm.
Quack, quack!

The Horse

I am a horse.
I have long, strong legs
and a beautiful mane and tail.
I can walk and trot.
Sometimes, I even gallop!
I am the fastest animal
on the farm.
Neigh! Neigh!

The Sheep

I am a sheep.
My fur is called fleece.
If you give me a haircut,
you can use my thick wool
to make your own wool coat.
Ba-a-ah! Ba-a-ah!

The Rabbit

I am a rabbit.
I have very soft fur
and two long ears.
My tiny nose wiggles
all the time —
even when I eat clover
and carrots.
Nibble, nibble, crunch!

Please visit our Web site at: www.garethstevens.com
For a free color catalog describing Gareth Stevens Publishing's
list of high-quality books and multimedia programs, call
1-800-542-2595 (USA) or 1-800-387-3178 (Canada).
Gareth Stevens Publishing's fax: (414) 332-3567.

Library of Congress Cataloging-in-Publication Data

Lambilly-Bresson, Elisabeth de.
   [A la ferme. English]
   Animals on the farm / Elisabeth de Lambilly-Bresson. — North American ed.
      p. cm. — (Animal show and tell)
   ISBN-13: 978-0-8368-7834-9 (lib. bdg.)
    1. Domestic animals—Juvenile literature. I. Title.
 SF75.5.L3313   2007
 636—dc22   2006032932

This edition first published in 2007 by
Gareth Stevens Publishing
A Member of the WRC Media Family of Companies
330 West Olive Street, Suite 100
Milwaukee, WI 53212 USA

Translation: Gini Holland
Gareth Stevens editor: Gini Holland
Gareth Stevens art direction and design: Tammy West

This edition copyright © 2007 by Gareth Stevens, Inc. Original edition copyright © 2002 by
Mango Jeunesse Press. First published as *Les animinis: À la ferme* by Mango Jeunesse Press.

Printed in the United States of America

1 2 3 4 5 6 7 8 9 10 10 09 08 07 06